What Do You Mean When You Say Green?

And Other Poems of Color

What Do You Mean When You Say Green?

And Other Poems of Color

Poems by

Lori Levy

© 2023 Lori Levy. All rights reserved.
This material may not be reproduced in any form, published,
reprinted, recorded, performed, broadcast,
rewritten or redistributed without
the explicit permission of Lori Levy.
All such actions are strictly prohibited by law.

Cover image by Avi Levy
Author photo by Nao Kanai

ISBN: 978-1-63980-423-8

Kelsay Books
502 South 1040 East, A-119
American Fork, Utah 84003
Kelsaybooks.com

For Ma—Enid/Esther Sobel—who responded enthusiastically to the silly poems I wrote in second grade and is still, at age 90, cheering me on.

Thank you to all the members of my family, from the youngest to the oldest, and to my friends for their love and support. Apologies for not naming you individually.

Acknowledgments

These poems (or longer versions of some of them) have been published in the following journals and anthologies:

Angela Poetry Magazine: "I Fly to Israel for My Mother's 84th Birthday"
The Aurorean: "New Prayer," "Spice"
Blue Heron Review: "Before and After"
Blue Unicorn: "Craving"
borrowed solace: "The Chapter on Dry"
CAIRN: The St. Andrews Review: "In the Mood for Orange"
The Cape Rock: "What's in a Rose?"
Dear Mr. President, Journal of Modern Poetry #21: "Where Are the Purples?"
The Examined Life Journal: "Black Toes"
International Poetry Review: "Funky Fuchsia"
Jewish Journal: "Funky Fuchsia"
Littoral Magazine: "At My Father's Funeral," "First Time in Playa Venao, Panama," "Panama Gray"
MacGuffin: "Black Eyes"
Nimrod International Journal: "Check-Up in Beer Sheva," "When Our Guest Makes Breakfast"
The Orange Room Review: "While Hiking"
The Penn Review: "Tongue-Tied"
Persimmon Tree: "Purple Yams"
The Poeming Pigeon: "True or False"
Poetry East: "Broadening the Spectrum," "To the Self-Help Authors I've Been Reading Lately"
Psychological Perspectives: "What Do You Mean When You Say Green?"
Quiddity: "Elephant Day"
Quill and Parchment Magazine: "I Fly to Israel for My Mother's 84th Birthday," "The Golden Years"
SISTERS SINGING, Incantations, Blessings, Chants, Prayers and Sacred Stories from Women Writers: "The Blue Embrace"

Surprised by Joy: "Morning Walk," "Thank You, Ma" (previously published as "Pink Berries")
The Times of Israel (The Blogs): "Torah in the Fields"
Voices Israel: "The Blue Embrace," "Little Surprises"
Wilda Morris's Blog: "When Our Guest Makes Breakfast"
Your Daily Poem: "Almost," "In the Mood for Orange," "Simple Things," "Spice," "What Do You Mean When You Say Green?"

Awards

"When Our Guest Makes Breakfast" won 1st Place in the March 2021 Poetry Challenge on the subject of fruit for Wilda Morris's blog.

"Funky Fuchsia" won 2nd Place in Wilda Morris's 2023 Poetry Challenge on the theme of color.

"I Fly to Israel for My Mother's 84th Birthday" won 1st Place in the Angela Poetry Contest in 2017.

Contents

What Do You Mean When You Say Green?	13
The Blue Embrace	14
Simple Things	15
Craving	16
Spice	17
In the Mood for Orange	18
Little Surprises	19
What's in a Rose?	20
New Prayer	21
Funky Fuchsia	22
When Our Guest Makes Breakfast	23
Morning Walk	24
Before and After	25
Almost	26
I Fly to Israel for My Mother's 84th Birthday	27
Check-Up in Beer Sheva	28
Torah in the Fields	29
First Time in Playa Venao, Panama	30
Tongue-Tied	31
Thank You, Ma	32
At My Father's Funeral	33
Purple Yams	34
Where Are the Purples?	35
True or False	36
The Chapter on Dry	37
The Golden Years	38
While Hiking	40
White on White	41
Black Eyes	42
Black Toes	44
Pink or Black	45
Elephant Day	46
Panama Gray	47

Broadening the Spectrum	48
To the Self-Help Authors I've Been Reading Lately	49
Gray Is the Color of—	50

What Do You Mean When You Say Green?

Do you mean the obvious, green as in grass?
Is it the green of a lawn well-kept
or the duller shade of a yellowing yard?
Are you thinking jungles, banana leaves?
Or is it a far-away dusty green—
a cactus in the desert or tumbleweed?

Perhaps you mean something else entirely:
green as in money, green with envy,
green as in *go* in a traffic light.

Maybe the mold on a piece of bread.
Color of decay, rusting copper.
Tint of your skin when you're feeling queasy.

What if my green is lighter than yours:
mint or lime or avocado
when you are fixed on fir or cypress?
Will we be able to blend our greens?
Compromise on a Kelly green?

If you say green to me tonight,
will you be thinking of a tattooed hip?
Craving scoops of pistachio ice cream?
Or can I assume your green will mean
the flecks you see in my hazel eyes?

The Blue Embrace

I am here on the garden swing
lazing in the sun on the same spot
where the cat lay curled up in dreams
of clouds and embryonic peace
before I came,
but, please, don't look for me now.

I am entering the cat's world for a while,
losing myself in the scent of eucalyptus leaves,
resting, with unhurried grace,
under skies pregnant with treetops
and the flapping wings of birds,
dreaming of the gentle Mother's
silent, blue embrace.

I am concentrating on the cat now—
not on its departure,
but on the absence of its calm repose—
and I wish not to be disturbed
when I am feeling myself into a soft ball of fur
and shutting out everything but

the sun penetrating my hungry pores,
the leaves whispering their lullabies to me,
and the wind breathing like a lover on my closed lids—
and blowing my weariness into the heavens
where it is caught and converted into
birdsong, heart-piercing and eternal.

Simple Things

In my mother's sunroom on Kibbutz Revivim
we hear the cows and the birds.
One bird, whose name I don't know,
trills the same notes over and over
the way my mother, at 90, repeats the same comments,
same questions, same quiet awe: *Once I had a good memory.*
I took care of you all. Is it time for lunch?
Do we know what's for supper? The sky is so blue.
The wind is blowing out there. And always, always,
It's important to laugh and to laugh at yourself.
She tells us again how she and my father met
in the Honor Society in Weequahic High School in Newark.
Sometimes, out of nowhere, a song pops up
from her childhood, every word remembered as she sings
Down by the Old Mill Stream,
I Love Coffee, I Love Tea,
My Country Tis of Thee.

Light pours in through the windows in the sunroom.
We fill with warmth. Pink bougainvilleas brush the windows,
a lemon tree before us, family photos on the walls and in frames
on the bookshelves: weddings, babies. My father's paintings.
In the sunroom beside my 90-year-old mother,
I feel cradled, held. This is peace, I think.
No expectations, no judgments anymore.
Just a being in the moment, in the comfort
of the same questions, the same answers.
Like meditation, says my nephew.
I probe her for tips about love and life.
The sky is so blue, she says. It is, it is.
I wait for her to remind me it's important to laugh.

Craving

Mid-September and I crave color,
red as Bloody Mary spilled on maple leaves;

want the wind to slam me back
into an orange mouth
with bright seductive tongues;

want the fever that lights up the sky
to light me up, too,
make me delirious enough
to sing *Libiamo* on the chairlift
to the top of Mt. Stowe—

though, afterwards, I'll have
nothing to show but

a handful of leaves
pressed like dried desire
between the pages of my book

and a paper bag full
of McIntoshes, so tart
they make me cry.

Spice

It's the time of year I want to be there, not here:
back east, where the hills flush red as guilt,
as if a secret has been exposed.
But there is no secret, just October
in Vermont. Saffron, turmeric,
chili pepper on the leaves.

It's taken years for me to notice;
only now I can admit
that here, too, the trees break out
in spicy salsa flames—
though it's our winter that sizzles:
November and December
when liquid ambers blaze as brightly
as the maples I have yearned for.
Too long I've missed the scarlet
of crepe myrtles in L.A. . . .

not just leaves turning red,
not paprika, sweet or hot,
but the glow they spark in me—
and whatever in that fervor feels
like revelry, rebellion.
Something fierce unleashed
makes me blush like those hills.

In the Mood for Orange

I want to discover what's orange in the world:
to come upon a leopard lily,
flame lichen clinging to a rock.
A barn swallow's chest, a monarch's wing.
Or just a bird-of-paradise against the sky.

I could slice a mango or suck on a section
of tangerine. Make soup for lunch
with pumpkin, squash, carrots, yams.
Could settle down by a fire, copper and blue,
or by the orange glow of a glass lamp.

What I have in mind is a fat ripe sun
the scarlet of a California poppy—
and me in an ocher-orange dress,
lips painted mandarin, twirling
to the rattle of Mexican maracas

until I drop like the sun
and the world grows dark again.

Little Surprises

Today I see red flowers dancing by the dusty roadside,
a brown bird hopping on a garbage can lid—
just as joyful as the one in the tree. Funny,
because on the same path yesterday,
I saw only the dust, the garbage, and the fog.

What's in a Rose?

She hates roses, she says.
Roses are chapels and cemeteries,
the smell of funerals and viewing rooms,
bouquets around an open casket,
dozens and dozens—and her mother
pumped with embalming fluids,
rouge painted on her hardened cheeks,
a rosary wrapped around her stiff, ungiving hand.
Bright blooms all around
her mother.
Before that, too: red, pink, white
for her three old aunts in Chicago,
the petals she had flung on their coffins.
Not a scent she would dab behind her ears,
not a gift she might place in a glass vase on her mantel.
No gleam in her eyes or soft moan in her throat
at the sight of a single long-stemmed rose—
like the one my husband brought in,
fresh from the garden,
opening its burgundy velvet
deep and wide as a ripening
woman.

New Prayer

Forget health and peace and happiness.
Let's try a new prayer.

Hurl us headfirst into reds and blues,
tomatoes and pizzas, mountains and sky,
and tongues the color of blue Popsicles.
Give us tulips and fir trees, oranges, shade.
Plunge us like the sun for a dip in the sea.
Let us melt and cool, sweat and shiver.

And a special request: put a deer in my chest,
wild berries in my legs,
and I want, for once, an oregano smile,
not pearls or diamonds or a Mona Lisa.
Let me fly in circles and not make sense.
Let me look at the world with spice in my lips.

Rouse us, when we fall, with spearmint leaves
and shine us well with olive oil.
Kiss us to brilliance, kiss us to life.
Scatter blessings like bird seed all over the planet.

Thank you, thank you for being such a sport.
And now would you join us in another game?—
a green and white day with pink on the edges.
The board is open, we've returned to Start.

Funky Fuchsia

Friday nights at my mother-in-law's
I follow the exquisite nails
of my Armenian sister-in-law from Iran.
Pale blue sometimes like her mohair sweater,
or yellow, pushing back a strand of dark hair.
Burgundy on the white bread she raises
to her lips at the evening meal;
funky fuchsia under the water in the kitchen sink.
Five cool kiwis hold a glass of tea.
Classic reds flirt with the tip of a cigarette.

Fingernails like castanets that click behind her words,
like sparks that fly beside her stories of Tehran.
Nails that give a shape to laughter,
come alive like drops of Jasmine,
who dyes T-shirts in America—
teal green, ruby red, juniper berry.

When Our Guest Makes Breakfast

It's not that I'm bored with toast and jam,
just that our guest has sliced a papaya
for breakfast this morning, and those red-orange slivers,
flushed and wet, lie curled on a plate
in the center of our table, offering themselves.

Just that I'm drawn to his hand on the knife,
the grace of his wrist as he peels and carves,
drawn to this blaze of mango, papaya—
and the speckled green kiwi
he tosses on top like a handful of coins.

Not that I yearned for a taste of the tropics
or favor pulp over toasted rye,
just that—this moment—I cannot resist
the cactus pear on the edge of the plate

that he's pared and opened
and placed within reach of my fingers.

Morning Walk

The point is to focus.
I could begin with my socks. Texture. Weave.
Thickness of cotton against the bottoms of my feet.
My mind pulls me this way and that way
like a frisky dog yanking at its leash.
Why socks? it wants to know. Why heels, toes
when a single red geranium hangs from a balcony
on a brown stucco building across the street?
And why a single bloom when faced with such abundance
of color and scent? Jasmine, white roses, lemon trees, oranges.
How can I concentrate on the bright, pocked skin
of the fruit on those branches? I am thirsty. I prefer to imagine
orange juice, ice, a tall glass of coldness
I can hold in my hand. So delicious to invent. To drift away
to the *not* here, to glasses I can almost hear clinking
at a party I wasn't at—in a Greek restaurant
where my son played guitar.

Back to socks, shoes pressing down, shadows on the pavement
of ficus leaves. Adirondack chairs beckon
from porches and lawns, always in twos,
always empty, tempting me to sit and
rest for a while. I am thirsty, this city is thirsty,
yards yellowing in L.A., some almost bald.
More and more landscapes of gravel and wood chips,
cactus, deer grass. Whatever will survive.

Is focus the point? Or is it something else?
I thank my socks for taking me on this journey.
For cushioning, absorbing. For being what they are:
soft and white, like the roses I pass—
and worn in places, like the paint on the picket fences.

Before and After

Silence had a different feel before.
Used to hang in our back yard
infecting flowers, trees, and grass,
blunting, blurring, muting
till all took on a flattened tone.
A presence, sheer but unmistakable,
that left its mark upon the world—
no human sound beyond our hedge.

Now the silence has a sheen.
Seems to polish every leaf,
draw attention to what's there—
date and palm, cypress, fig.
Leaves like spikes or fans or hearts.
What was merely green before
now is tinged with blue or purple,
but mostly with a glow of yellow.
The yard that seemed so empty once
grows fuller by the day,
rich as fuchsia bougainvillea.

Look how this *after* garden blooms.
How fertile this new peace.

Almost

It's an almost day—
almost perfect, almost nothing missing:
the sky a pure untainted blue,
just what I want on this particular afternoon,
the garden glowing its green at me
while the bold pink petals of the bougainvillea
in a brilliant merging of chaos and order
hang with ease from the sumac tree.
The blaze of fuchsia in the corner of our yard
has sparked some flames on the date palm, too.

But no one beside me on the garden swing—
just when I'm wishing someone were here
to fill the empty spot on the cushion.
To swing in that barely perceptible way
while, silent or not,
we sip together on ice water
freshened with cucumber slices,
though it's more about the hand on the glass
than the drink itself.
About a friend to witness this scene with me—
a backdrop for us
while we speak of things
unrelated to beauty.

I Fly to Israel for My Mother's 84th Birthday

We celebrate in the hills. My sisters spread blankets
on a grassy slope in the Forest of Angels,
Ya'ar Hamalakhim, and there, under pines and oaks—
our parents on beach chairs that seem to float away
in a sea of wildflowers—we feast on the lunch they've laid out
on a table in the clearing: lasagna and quiche,
schnitzel, potatoes, salads, fresh peppers.
No balloons at this party, but we have bright red
anemones, clusters of pink columbine, white-pink asphodel,
tangles of mustard weed, yellow and green,
and down below, in the valley, the woolly backs of sheep
that a Bedouin has brought to graze on the tall grass,
their *maaing* and *baaing* blending with the Arabic music
blaring from a radio nearby, where a group of men,
hands on each other's shoulders, bodies linked,
kick their legs, slide this way and that way,
marking the beat that echoes through the trees—
while we chatter and laugh, our parents surrounded
by their children, grandchildren, great-grandchildren,
and I think: this is what I want, too,
a birthday party outdoors when I'm 84,
no walls around me, just a spot with a view,
sun warming my wrinkled cheek
while I gaze with pleasure at the family we've produced,
my husband at my side, details beginning to blur perhaps—
but what will that matter if I can have a moment
of lasagna in the woods, cake and wildflowers and a birthday song
filled with the moaning of sheep and squeals of revelry
and, clear and emphatic and ever-present, my mother's voice,
reminding me once again that it's important to laugh,
at ourselves, our lives.

Check-Up in Beer Sheva

I ask about her check-up, if everything went well.
Yes, says my sister, and tells me about the doctor—
how friendly he was, the gynecologist in Beer Sheva,
how he asked about her work, said it sounded interesting,
which caught her by surprise, made her want to laugh
because what's so interesting about checking tomatoes?

I want to know more. What exactly does she do
at the Desert Agro Research Center near her kibbutz?
I probe like a gynecologist, shining my light
in the dark, on the details, as if tomatoes grow like
polyps on a cervix. I picture her bending to a vine
beneath a blue sky, rows and rows of them
sprouting from the sand in the Negev desert.
No, she says. She inspects them in the lab—after they've been
picked, sorted, stored for a week or two in the fridge.
She must feel each one: is it firm, flexible, soft?
Is there rot? Are there cracks, color defects?
Are they getting enough salt? Tomatoes grow smaller
and sweeter in salt water pumped in from
underground aquifers. She checks peppers, too.
Cucumbers, dates, basil, mint. Counts the seeds in the eggplants.
Examines the strawberries: are their shoulders white?
I smile at this—how lovely to think that strawberries have
shoulders, pale above their red gowns!

This is her job. Bright red tomatoes. Pomegranates,
olives—and her favorite, sweet bite peppers, red, yellow, orange,
sweeter than strawberries according to her tests.
She takes home baskets of color and freshness. My mouth aches
for the crunch of peppers. *Maybe,* says my sister, *it's more
interesting to check tomatoes than vaginas every day.*

Torah in the Fields

Not you, but your question
has flown with me to Israel.
What makes it a Bar Mitzvah?
There's no rabbi, no synagogue, no Torah.
I see your point, Mother-in-law.
And now I also see poppies.
Yes, the poppies are out.
Mazal Tov! Mazal Tov! they call to my nephew
when we pass them on the trail in northern Galilee.
They are swaying, nodding,
deep in prayer and celebration.
Time to break out and bloom;
vibrant, red, they applaud *thirteen*.

The cows have come, too. Are they not like rabbis?—
showing us the way. They are everywhere:
on the hills, in the caves, the streams.
They leave warnings on the trail: where *not* to step.
This way, they say, higher and higher up the cliffs of Arbel,
and my nephew follows. The Kinneret shines below,
and in the water, his reflection: boy becoming man.

Later, in Ein Karem, we bless him in a garden
where grapes were once pressed into wine.
The steaks on the barbecue know this is a Bar Mitzvah.
They conspire with the stones in the courtyard,
the arches, the peeling walls, beautiful as frescoes;
with the lemons and the grapevine, the pink flowers
of the Judas tree—all of them whispering about
the *mitzvahs* of this boy whom we have gathered to honor
around a table bursting with fresh and tender and
sweet on a sunny day in Jerusalem.

First Time in Playa Venao, Panama

This place seduces you.
If not love at first sight,
then a wooing day by day
as the *holas,* the smiles, seep into you,
the waves roll in, the wooden swings beckon
on the shore. And, ahh, the colors,
how they draw you in: houses painted pink
or green, turquoise, peach.
You begin to ripen like the coconuts
above you in the trees,
soften like the mangoes, the bananas.
Soon you slow to the pace
of chickens strolling, fearless, in the road,
cows grazing in the field.
A pace of wonder, of taking in what's there,
as when two horses seem to come from nowhere
to munch in the yard
outside the house in the jungle
where you're staying.
How can you resist this place
when everywhere you look—on the beach, on patios
in front of shops, restaurants, homes—
hammocks hang and tempt you
to stop rushing,
stop whatever else you're doing?
Come, each hammock seems to whisper,
lie down in my embrace.
Rock a little.
Fall in love.

Tongue-Tied

I am tongue-tied in the hospital,
can't think what to say to the face above the neck
with the tracheotomy tube. Her lips ask how we are—
her children, grandchildren, great-grandson.
Perhaps I've never been a storyteller,
but here in this room, where life is about
blood sugar, oxygen, catheters,
my stories get shorter and shorter. She shrugs in response.
I begin to speak in initials: RN, RT, PMV.
Every day the same words: yogurt, water.
The same tired questions: Did she eat? Is she in pain?

I need color in this space. Fragrance. Tang.
Pine trees, eucalyptus, lavender, lemons.
I need crunchy new words, bites of apples.
Or dark chocolate ones that resonate with cellos.
I want to make something up.
Fabricate. Exaggerate—especially in pink.
Maybe tell her, if she gets off the bed,
if she walks to the window, she'll see
cherry trees blooming, millions of blossoms
lifting in the breeze, like a troupe of ballerinas
in pink tutus. Bubbles of Bazooka filling and filling
till—just before they pop—they freeze into ice cream,
scoops of raspberry or pink peppercorn
with pomegranate seeds. I want to smooth it on her cheeks.
Make her glow again.

But, of course, I just stare out her window
into gray cement walls. *Are you hungry?* I ask.
The yogurt I feed her is cherry-flavored,
the rash on her body, a rosy pink.

Thank You, Ma

It's you, Ma, who knows how to look
at dry brown grass, thorny bushes,
who walks with delight through chaparral,
pointing to the tiny pink berries
on a dull green shrub beside the trail.

At My Father's Funeral

We are lucky: the sun comes out
when we bury my father, a welcome warmth
in this colder than usual winter in Israel

as though he's arranged this for us,
still warming, protecting us.

The day after the funeral the sky
begins to cry, pouring and pouring
like those who wail and beat their chests
in grief. I should be the sky, should be
sobbing at the loss of my beloved father,
but it seems I am the desert
that surrounds his kibbutz: my eyes are dry.

Will the tears come later?

Sometimes rain fills the wadis,
and the desert becomes a torrent, roads flooded, blocked.
Now it is *the season,* the time of year when
life bursts from the sand, buds opening, blossoming.
On Saturday the roads are jammed:
carloads of people coming out for no other reason than
to gaze at pink, yellow, red, purple flowers
and to picnic among them. How can I cry

when I can't feel his absence?
When my father is blooming in my heart,
vibrant as the anemones that paint the dunes red,
the whole land on fire.

Purple Yams

Our debts are magical: they keep growing and growing
like the beans Jack planted in his mother's garden.
We, too, look for a castle in the sky,
but instead of a hen who lays golden eggs,
we glimpse the boot of the giant, stamping, crushing.

Another bill unpaid or paid partially or late.
The world shrinks to the size of a coin; my life,
the constant counting of what I have or don't have.
I inhale scarcity, exhale scarcity.
It settles on my tongue, sharp as complaint.
Whines in my ears. Crawls like an itch along my skin.

So I borrow my son's Discman and go to bed with a professor—
his voice soothing me, teaching me Mindfulness, Meditation.
Focus on your breath, he says. *Observing without judging.*
I close my eyes, pay attention to my breathing,
how it carries me away—to my son's friend.
To her laughter and her long, black hair. My breathing turns to
cocoa: I am sipping the Mexican hot chocolate
she makes us one evening, cinnamon-flavored,
cool whip on top. And now I'm biting into
hopia, the Filipino pastries she buys for us,
flaky, filled with yams, purple yams. *Ube.*
I am savoring the sweetness, mesmerized by that purple,
how it lures me to meadows of iris and lavender, speaks to me
of amethyst. Of emperors in long robes.
Hopia, I murmur. Like a chant, a mantra. *Hopia. Hopia.*

I open my eyes. My husband lies beside me in the semi-dark room,
a spot of light on the wall where the nightlight casts its glow.
I see purple in the shadows.

Where Are the Purples?

There we are on the map: not we the People,
but we the Reds, we the Blues.
We speak our minds, protest, wave signs or flags,
the gulf between us growing wider and wider.

How can we compromise when we're so damn sure
we're right, they're wrong? Where are the Purples?
Welcoming, inclusive. The ones who
gaze into each other's eyes, see themselves
in the other, all of us the same.
But, no, we are the Reds, the Blues. There is no middle.
Compromise is curled up sick on our latest bridge.
Beaten and battered from all sides.
Broken. Dying. Cursed like something dirty.

The *what* doesn't matter. Could be guns
we're talking about. Health care. Immigration.
We stamp our feet. Dig in. The gap grows wider.
Doesn't matter *who*. All we know is
someone has to go. Keep these people in,
kick those jerks out, and our problems will be solved.

Compromise collapses in the middle of a bridge,
desperate to be nursed back to life.
Straining to catch a glimpse of Trust,
its only hope. Where is Trust?
Not with us, the Reds, the Blues —
but surely it's still there, warm and alive,
beating in the hearts of the Purples.

True or False

I don't want to argue, but what do we do
when my true is your false,
when we each think the other is wrong,
dangerously wrong?
When we can't find the middle
between your beliefs and mine—
the middle so barren nothing grows there but
suspicion, shadowy and dark as distrust,
and we can't even agree on the purpose of a mask
that I wear to protect and you resent
as a loss of freedom.

Can we agree on anything? Please tell me it's true:
the beauty of an oak's yellow leaves,
shimmers of gold in the afternoon sun.
Tell me you love sour on your tongue:
a squeeze of lemon. Chicken piccata.
That you laugh with a child
who runs faster than you,
tickled by the joy of his or her pride.

Tell me you agree that true means
a bench where we can sit side by side,
wrapped in the glow of yellow oak leaves,
entertained by squirrels. No false
in the way they leap from branch to
branch, living their lives.

The Chapter on Dry

She's not just hiking; she's *reading* the canyon
as if it's a book offering clues to her life.
In this winter chapter she confronts the *dry:*
the cracked earth thirsting for water,
bare stalks along the trail
where yellow used to bloom, wild as passion.
She pulls at a twig, snaps it in half.
This is how marriage looks, she says,
when love is not present.
She points to the brown, the barren, the dead.
But then, as she turns a bend:
red berries on a tree and even there,
beneath the stalks, grass still green and vibrant.
She spies a blossom on a stem,
marvels at its glowing white petals,
warmed alive by the sun.
Evidence, she says, *of the power of love.*
And she can't ignore the late afternoon sky
with its orange-pink swirls, lush as desire—
though it's the violet she remarks on,
how it has slipped in and altered the blue.
By the end of the trail, she has
shifted her focus from thorn to bud.
The canyon is her prayer book:
she immerses herself, praising, extolling.

The Golden Years

I'd rather talk about pumpkin spiced latte
than aging. If anything's golden,
it's these 380 calories of sweetness I sip through a hole
in the lid of my cup when I order it for the first time
at LAX before my flight to Israel to see my sisters, brother,
nieces, nephews, and my parents, 86 and 87.

Who named them the golden years? Golden smells young,
like coconut oil. The gleam of lean muscles on a blanket
at the beach. I don't understand. Why not the walker years?
The bone-breaking years? *More like the rusty years,*
says my father. Corrosion, erosion. The daily strain
to see, hear, remember. To balance on tired legs,
the body no longer a friend. He notes one benefit:
no worries anymore about the long-term side effects
of medications. My mother models the new shirt I've brought her
and reminds us, in case we need reminding, it's important to laugh.

Late October now and the sun shines on two canes
slanting against their chairs in a restaurant at the beach
in Ashdod, where we take them for lunch, a table outside,
because they want to see the sea, haven't seen it for years.

At home, in the Negev desert, he grinds coffee beans,
and every day after lunch makes strong filtered coffee
from the beans she still orders from the shop in Jaffa.
Later, after dinner, they eat grapes, prunes, dates
and finish with espresso, sipping from cups they bought once
in Italy, perhaps, or received from loved ones.
They pour some for me. We talk and pause, drink, listen.
I begin to believe that, as the body shrinks,
the self expands. Raw, exposed, it opens like a gift
to any who will receive it, offering its gold,

collected over years: nuggets that come to me now
with the gentle savoring of black and bitter—
surely as good as pumpkin spiced latte
slurped through a lid before boarding a flight.

While Hiking

I could easily have missed—
among the sycamores and pines—
the white shirt with the simple cut,
worn by a hiker walking briskly with her dog.

A shirt as plain as a daisy or the bark of a tree—
no sequins or see-through or lace—
but there it is, coming towards me
on the trail: the flow of cotton,
hanging on her curves like a picture on display.
Not a shout, but a whisper in the woods,
one that blends and belongs,
enhancing what it hides.

It's the language of stitch and form and art,
and just as I'm catching a phrase of it,
she rushes past and that's it:
among laurels and purple sage,
a glimpse of something as fleeting
as the flash of white on a deer's tail.

White on White

We have been living in limbo
for a year,
neither here nor there,
hanging on to old ideas,
old colors: bright
embroidered pillows,
paintings laughing with reds and yellows,
Persian rugs, rich as wine,
plants creeping up and down walls.

But our new house refuses
to come alive,
refuses to take on the shape
of the old one, an ocean
and continent away.
Pale maple wood furniture here.
White couch, blank walls,
a carpet too light to hide
even the barest water stains.

Only the bedroom looks full and ripe,
a burgundy chenille blanket
draped luxuriously over the bed,
like a long, drawn-out
exclamation of joy.

Or have we simply
redefined our colors?—
created a new scene:
white on white,
like a woman without make-up.
A beautiful woman.

Black Eyes

The black eyes of taxi drivers
follow me down the streets
of Jerusalem
where I get lost in smells
of pizza, *shawarma,*
fresh-baked cakes with names
like Mozart and Black Forest.

It is enough
to walk these streets again;
to drink a cold glass
of fresh-squeezed orange juice
from a corner stand
on Ben Yehuda Street,
where a soldier with an M-16
slung over his shoulder
downs carrot juice
in the mid-afternoon heat.

Strands of cigarette smoke
pull me forward
through narrow alleys
with white stone walls,
past the checkered heads
of Arabs in *keffiyehs,*
and the black coats of men
who flash by in droves
on their way to prayers.

If you were with me,
we'd buy peanuts for me
and sunflower seeds for you
to crack between your teeth
on the streets of your childhood.

You'd slip coins into the cup
of a one-legged beggar
who's sat on the same sidewalk spot
on Jaffa Street for thirty years.

I am alone this time,
but I drop five shekels
into the open case
of a Russian violinist
pouring *Polovtsian Dances*
into the promenade.

The news is everywhere—
in the arms of the violinist,
in the black eyes of the city.
Another soldier killed
on the Lebanese border.

On a bench in a courtyard
you showed me once,
I eat falafel
and watch the sun light up
the kerchief of an old woman
peeling potatoes on a balcony.
Laundry flaps on clotheslines,
and from an open window
wails the black-eyed voice
of Boaz Sharabi on the radio.
Sometimes, it is enough
to be alive.

Black Toes

I try not to stare at her rotting black toes
sticking out of the hospital sheets.
One machine helps her breathe;
another empties waste from her blood.
This is my mother-in-law: a body on a bed,
bloated, fractured. A weight to be turned
and propped. A back with a stage-four bedsore.
Bones like cheese, the surgeon says,
but, against all odds, she has survived the surgery.
Now infection holds her hostage:
she sleeps, heart barely beating.
A nurse pries her eyelids open, slips in her drops.
Can she see us through the fog?
Is she there behind the silence?

Two and a half years she's lived in bed,
suffering and in pain—but holding on to what was left:
eyes that could still watch the chefs
on the food channel, though her ears had stopped hearing;
a mouth, an appetite for the meals on her tray—
and suddenly, these last few months, a craving for honey,
not in tea, but drizzled over chicken and rice, eggs and cake.
All along she's wanted time: another day,
another moment with her family. Nothing grand,
just the sweetness of a greeting or a smile,
a hand squeezing hers.

Black toes, closed eyes. Septic now. I sit by her side,
all the time thinking of my mother's words
when *her* mother died after years of Alzheimer's—
like a sigh I can't stifle, that line she kept quoting
from a poem she once read: *Finally the dead died.*

Pink or Black

I could choose black,
color of wasted time,
color of stuck-in-a-traffic-jam.
Or splatter some pink, for me living it up
in this slow-moving lane,
filling myself with Maori love songs,
dancing with natives on a mountaintop,
when I should be home, frying schnitzel.

Pink for this moment alone, foot on the gas,
for the crazy comfort of wheel and windshield,
for catching my breath between here and there
as I float along in a river of cars.
As I contemplate a line I heard,
or read, or wanted to say:
a thought to share before forgotten.

I could be doing something better,
throbbing and glowing, moaning on sheets,
but I'm here right now on the 405.
Here with the girl in the red Camaro
who's pouring her self into her cell phone:
a picture of laughter and animation
that's got me wishing I could hear through glass.

With the bearded man in the black Denali,
who has me wondering, as he passes by,
tires blending with dust and grease:
what color will he greet his wife tonight?

Elephant Day

I wish I could say I'm a hummingbird
pulsing above a trumpet vine
or maybe a deer in a moment of stillness
or even a cow lying in the pasture or
standing and chewing all day long.
But I am an elephant today,
plodding about from room to room,
heavy with wrinkles and sagging hide,
so sluggish and gray it takes all my strength
to lift my legs, one lump at a time.
Neither pausing nor resting, but stumbling forward,
nose to the ground, I probe the cracks
in search of something I have yet to discover.

What will I find?
A pounding, a stirring, a call from the wild?
Maybe only a distant rumble.
My feet are attuned to the slightest vibration,
and my giant ears are listening.

Panama Gray

It's the rainy season here
in Playa Venao: gray sea, gray sky.
I sit on the beach staring into gray.
Gloom, I call it, because it's *not*
the sunny blue sky I left in L.A.
What is this gloom? The dull, the bland—
if that's what it is—holds me still in my chair,
comforts in a faded-old-blanket way.
I begin to see color: silver, pale blue, olive green.
Listen: this gloom isn't shy—waves thundering, seething,
howler monkeys roaring in the trees.
Gloom, I call it, but it tastes like a smoothie
made from pineapples, mangoes, bananas.

I have chosen to come. Have come to help.
Some days that means arms, mine,
bleeding and bruised from my five-year-old granddaughter
who pinches and scratches. How can I blame her?
Or her three-year-old sister who wails,
wants Mama to come home
and stay forever and ever.
The split is bitter, sharp and stinging
as the bites of chitras.
I watch their Papa—my son—
make them pancakes in the morning
with blueberries and bananas. Maple syrup
drizzled on top. I think about sweet—
how we crave it, need it. How here, in Playa Venao,
I walk through rain and mud, if I have to,
for a slice of Fabi's home-made cake
at el Café de Acá at the edge of the jungle.

Broadening the Spectrum

She is learning about color,
not the pulsing scarlets that mark a life,
but the softer tones that define her day.
She welcomes beige:
color of being home together,
but working alone in different rooms.
Notes how it deepens to umber
when they sit side by side watching TV,
sienna when they turn to converse.
Some mornings begin with ash,
a dullness in the chest that threatens to
stain the space between them.
But she leaves it alone, trusts it to warm
as she lies beside him. To walnut, perhaps,
a brown that ripens in the curves of her arms,
mahogany as he reaches for her.
She believes in the flow, surrenders
to the shifting of currents
where shadows are enriched by tinges of purple
and new blends form
in the eddies.

To the Self-Help Authors I've Been Reading Lately

I get it. The choice is mine.
I can sit here worrying about this stack of bills
and the lack of funds to repair what's broken, leaking,
crumbling in house, car, body—or
I can inhale deeply, exhale slowly and
focus on this cup in my hand right here, right now.
Fear of what's coming or the warmth of coffee
sliding down my throat. I choose this mug
with its blue/brown/pink swirls that my grandchildren painted
in a ceramics shop. A birthday gift from them,
love scrawled on it. I rest my arms on the table, wood,
smooth as my face was before stress scratched lines on it.
Smooth as peanut butter, creamy, spread on
celery or bread. I choose this table,
light as wheat in a field or maize.
I could eat this color: quinoa, chick peas, tahini.
I could close my eyes and soak it in
through the tips of my fingers: a blandness that calms,
like a sandy beach. But my eyes are open,
and I notice now that this color is everywhere—
and that it blends with the pale tips of fronds
on the palms I glimpse through my window. With oak leaves,
drying, yellowing, preparing to fall.

White envelopes in a pile,
waiting to be opened—
and plum jam and the crunch of toast
as I chew.

Gray Is the Color of—

Once I told you I was in the mood for orange:
monarch's wing, mango, lips painted mandarin,
dancing to maracas at the setting of a fat ripe sun.

Gray is the color I crave today,
a rainy day kind of gray.

Color of lazy,
lying in bed
beneath a puffy blanket—
snuggling, cuddling
if not alone.

Color of comfort, curling up with a book,
coffee nearby, cookies on a plate.

Color of monotony, boredom—
or just a pause
from all the brightness, the noise.
A break from sunny blue skies.

Color of suffering—
or just a space to be, feel,
become a poem
tinged with hope
on a white page.

Color of compromise,
neither black nor white. A color to settle into,
like an armchair—like love
after the lust.

About the Author

Lori Levy's poems have appeared in *Rattle, Nimrod International Journal, Poet Lore, Paterson Literary Review, The MacGuffin,* and numerous other print and online literary journals and anthologies in the U.S., the U.K., and Israel. Her poems have also been published in medical humanities journals, including a hybrid piece (poetry/prose) she co-authored with her father, a physician. Her bilingual chapbook, *In the Mood for Orange,* was published in Israel in 2007. Lori lives with her extended family in Los Angeles, but "home" has also been Vermont and Israel and, for several months, Panama while visiting her son and granddaughters.

www.ingramcontent.com/pod-product-compliance
Lightning Source LLC
Chambersburg PA
CBHW031206160426
43193CB00008B/532